Space Voyager

Earth

by Vanessa Black

2/18

D0898711

Bullfrog
Books

Ideas for Parents and Teachers

Bullfrog Books let children practice reading informational text at the earliest reading levels. Repetition, familiar words, and photo labels support early readers.

Before Reading

- Discuss the cover photo. What does it tell them?

- Look at the picture glossary together. Read and discuss the words.

Read the Book

- "Walk" through the book and look at the photos. Let the child ask questions. Point out the photo labels.

- Read the book to the child, or have him or her read independently.

After Reading

- Prompt the child to think more. Ask: Earth is the only planet we know of that contains life. Why do you think this might be? What conditions does Earth have that make life possible?

Bullfrog Books are published by Jump!
5357 Penn Avenue South
Minneapolis, MN 55419
www.jumplibrary.com

Library of Congress Cataloging-in-Publication Data

Names: Black, Vanessa, 1973– author.
Title: Earth / Vanessa Black.
Description: Minneapolis, MN: Jump!, Inc., [2018]
Series: Bullfrog books. Space voyager
"Bullfrog Books are published by Jump!."
Audience: Ages 5–8. | Audience: K to grade 3.
Includes bibliographical references and index.
Identifiers: LCCN 2017023022 (print)
LCCN 2017024193 (ebook)
ISBN 9781624966835 (ebook)
ISBN 9781620318386 (hardcover: alk. paper)
ISBN 9781620318393 (pbk.)
Subjects: LCSH: Earth (Planet)—Juvenile literature.
Classification: LCC QB631.4 (ebook)
LCC QB631.4 .B58 2017 (print) | DDC 525—dc23
LC record available at https://lccn.loc.gov/2017023022

Editor: Jenna Trnka
Book Designer: Molly Ballanger
Photo Researchers: Molly Ballanger & Jenna Trnka

Photo Credits: Aphelleon/Shutterstock, cover; AlexRaths/iStock, 1; Samuel Borges Photography/Shutterstock, 3 (boy), 14; StepanPopov/Shutterstock, 3 (drawing); Ilike/Shutterstock, 4; MarcelClemens/Shutterstock, 5, 8–9, 23tr; BEST-BACKGROUNDS/Shutterstock, 6–7, 23tl; Triff/Shutterstock, 10; Darren Baker/Shutterstock, 11; Villiers Steyn/Shutterstock, 12–13; Dmitry Naumov/Shutterstock, 15; herjua/Shutterstock, 16–17; Vadim Sadovski/Shutterstock, 18–19, 23br; Artush/Shutterstock, 20–21; AlexHliv/Shutterstock, 23bl; KPG _ Payless/Shutterstock, 24.

Printed in the United States of America at Corporate Graphics in North Mankato, Minnesota.

Table of Contents

What is the third planet from the sun?

Here are some hints.

It is mostly water.

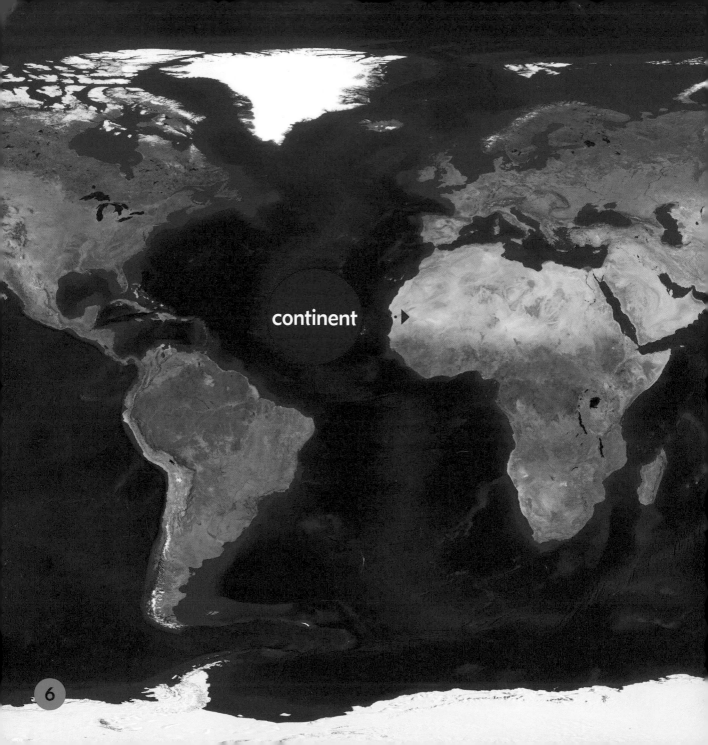

continent

It has continents.

It has one moon.

It is Earth!

moon

It spins.

This makes day and night.

The side that faces away from the sun is dark.

This is night.

The other side faces the sun.

It is day here.

11

It is the only planet known to have life.

Why?

It has air.
We need air to breathe.

14

It has water.

We need water to drink.

Do we know everything about Earth?

No.

There is a lot to learn.

We send out satellites.

They orbit Earth.

They send us pictures.

We explore the seas.
We learn more
every day!

A Look at Earth

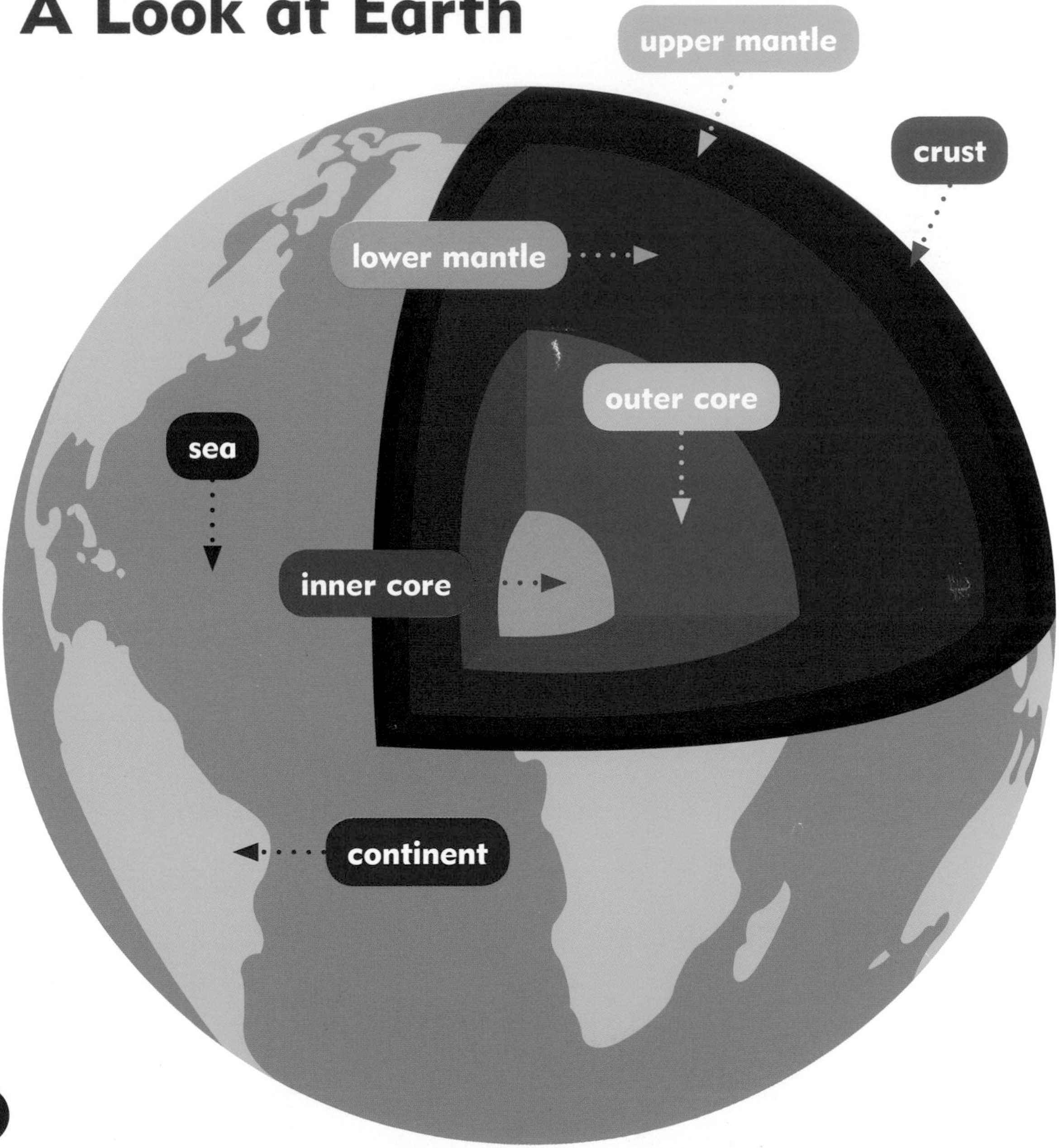

upper mantle

crust

lower mantle

outer core

sea

inner core

continent

Picture Glossary

continents
The seven large land masses on Earth.

planet
A large body that orbits the sun.

orbit
To travel around in circles.

satellites
Machines that orbit planets, the moon, and the sun.

Index

To Learn More

Learning more is as easy as 1, 2, 3.

1) Go to www.factsurfer.com

2) Enter "Earth" into the search box.

3) Click the "Surf" button to see a list of websites.

With factsurfer.com, finding more information is just a click away.